# CHRISTMAS STANDARDS

## 22 Jazzy and Fun Piano Arrangements

### ARRANGED BY MIKE SPRINGER

## CONTENTS

*For Jeff and Linda Patrick*

Produced by
Alfred Music
P.O. Box 10003
Van Nuys, CA 91410-0003
alfred.com

Printed in USA.

ISBN-10: 1-4706-4014-7
ISBN-13: 978-1-4706-4014-9

Cover Art:
Geometric Vector Pattern in Retro Style © Getty Images / Dudi-art •
Retro 50s Design Elements © Getty Images / Rach27 • Christmas Greeting Cards Collection © Getty Images / discan

# Auld Lang Syne

Traditional
Arr. Mike Springer

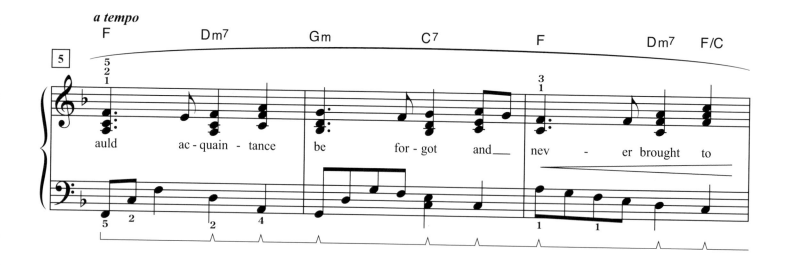

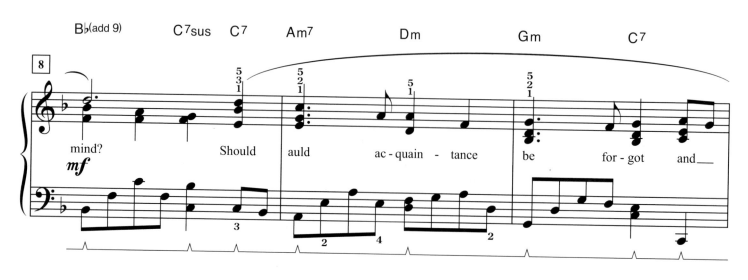

# Believe

*(from The Polar Express)*

Words and Music by
Alan Silvestri and Glen Ballard
Arr. Mike Springer

Moderately, with feeling

1. Chil - dren___ sleep - ing,___ snow is soft - ly fall - ing.___
2. Trains move___ quick - ly___ to their jour - ney's end.___

Dreams are call - ing___ like bells in the dis - tance.
Des - ti - na - tions___ are where we be - gin a - gain.

We were___ dream - ers___ not so long a - go,
Ships go___ sail - ing___ far a - cross the sea,

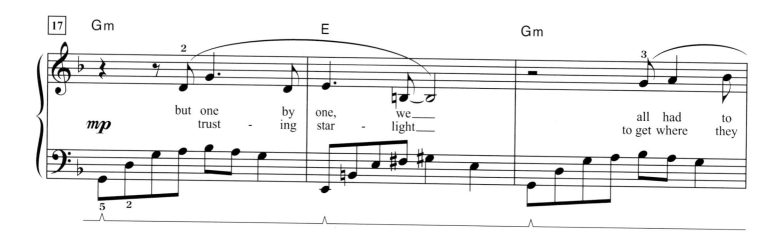

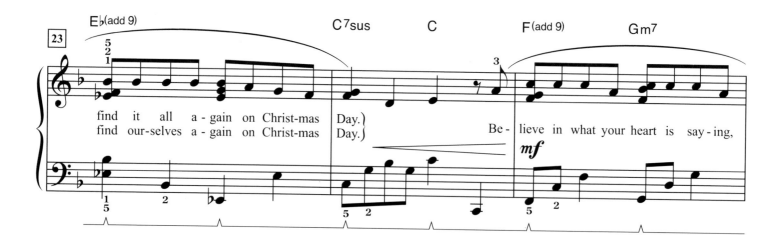

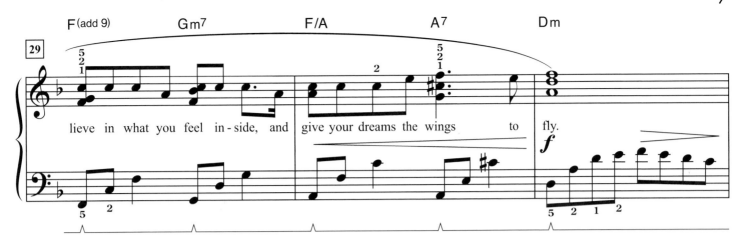

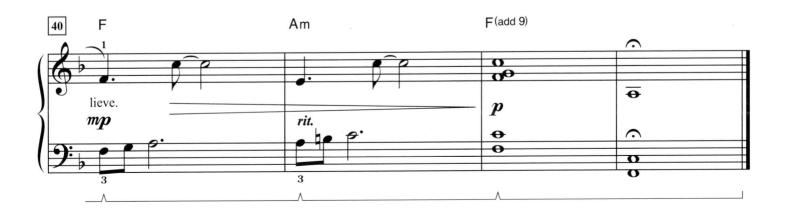

# Blue Christmas

Words and Music by
Bill Hayes and Jay Johnson
Arr. Mike Springer

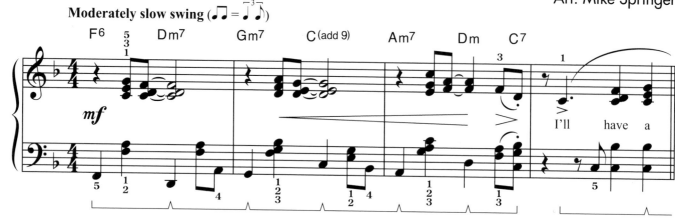

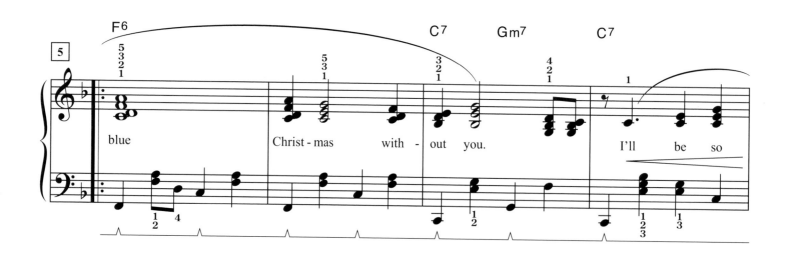

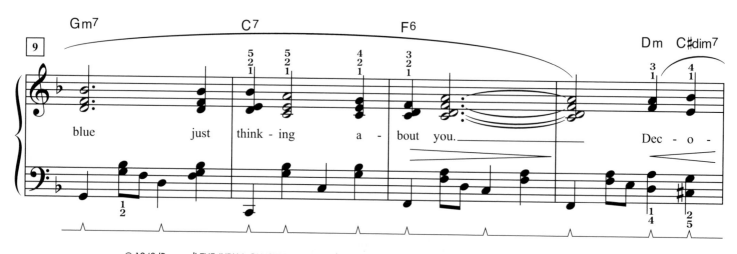

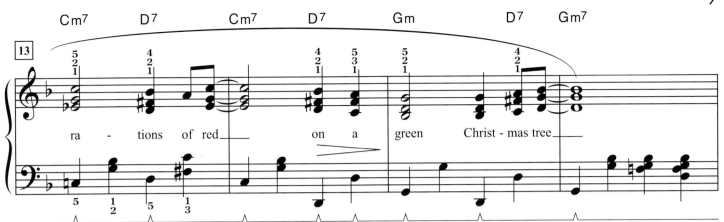

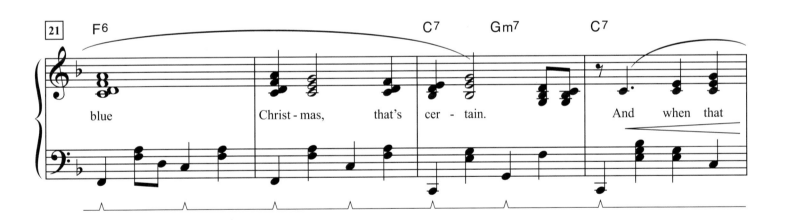

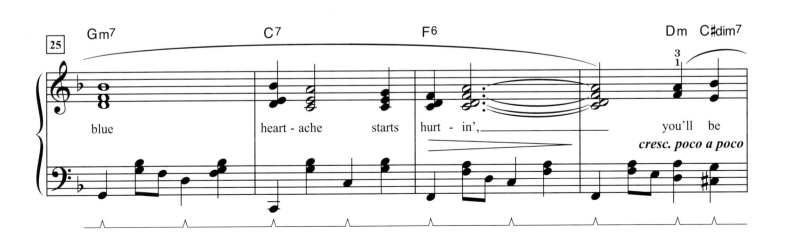

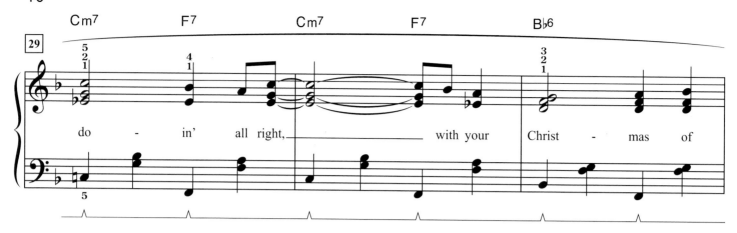

do - in' all right,_____ with your Christ - mas of

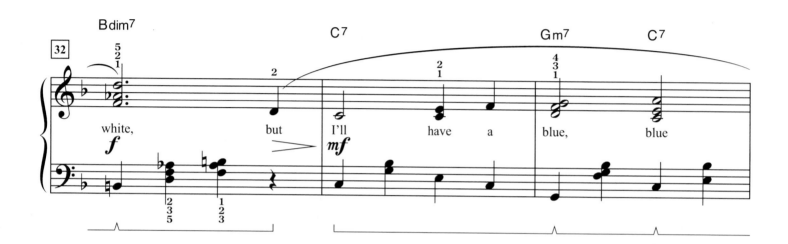

white, *f*    but    I'll    have    a    blue,    blue *mf*

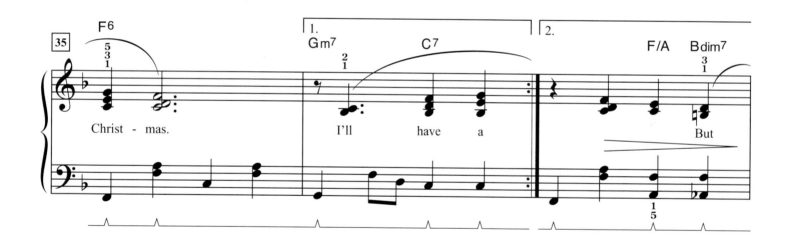

Christ - mas.    I'll    have    a    But

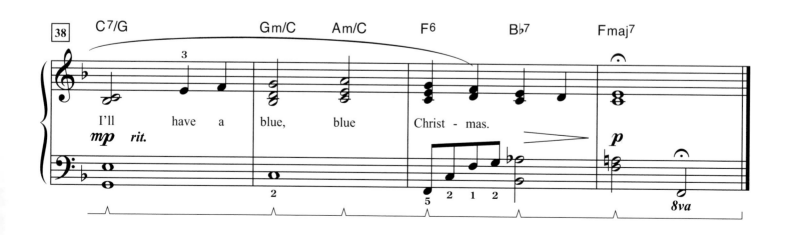

I'll    have    a    blue,    blue    Christ - mas.
*mp rit.*    *p*
*8va*

# Christmas Eve in My Home Town

Words and Music by Stan Zabka and Don Upton
Arr. Mike Springer

# Feliz Navidad

Words and Music by José Feliciano
Arr. Mike Springer

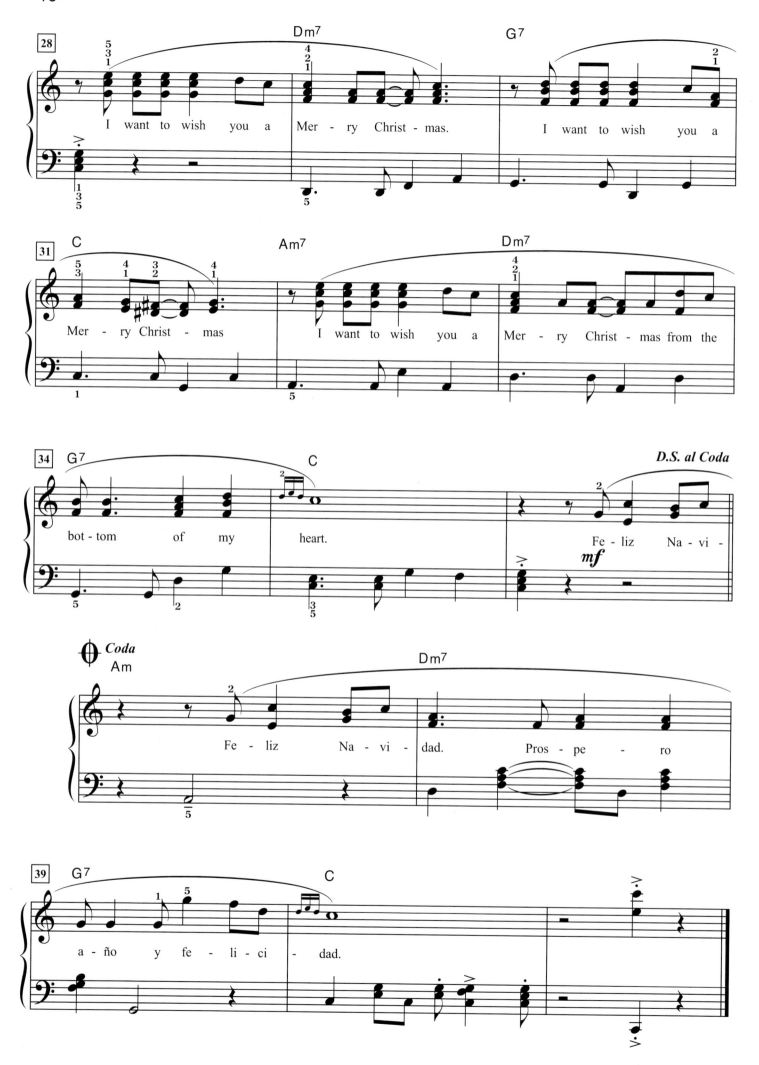

# Frosty the Snowman

Words and Music by
Steve Nelson and Jack Rollins
Arr. Mike Springer

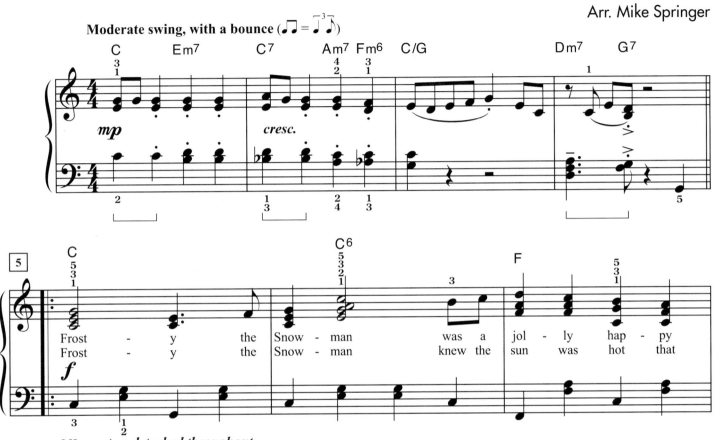

*LH quarters detached throughout*

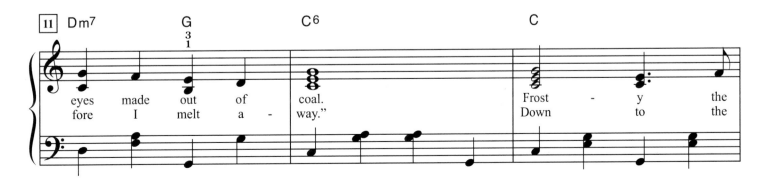

# Have Yourself a Merry Little Christmas

Words and Music by
Hugh Martin and Ralph Blane
Arr. Mike Springer

# A Holly Jolly Christmas

Words and Music by Johnny Marks
Arr. Mike Springer

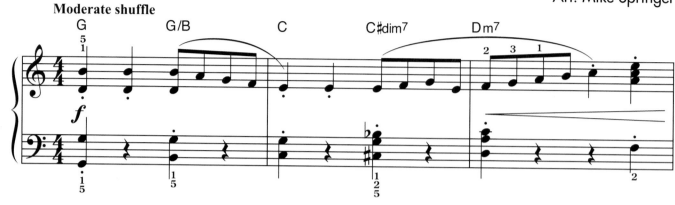

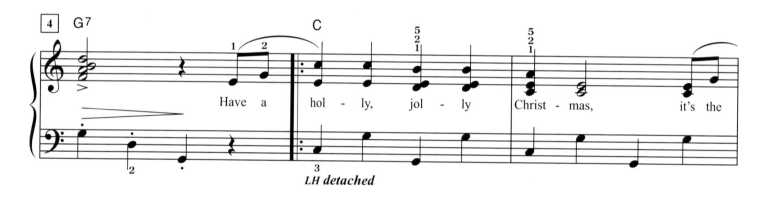

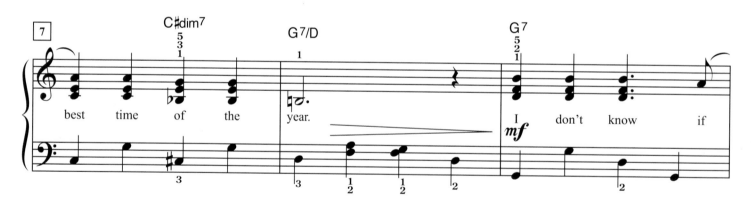

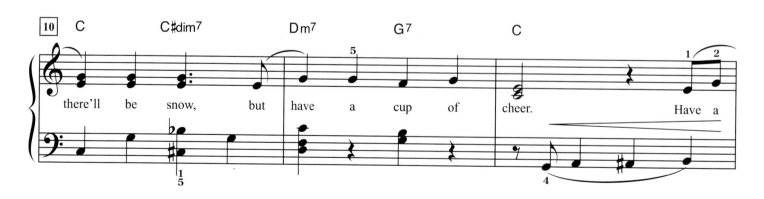

# (There's No Place Like)
# Home for the Holidays

Words by Al Stillman
Music by Robert Allen
Arr. Mike Springer

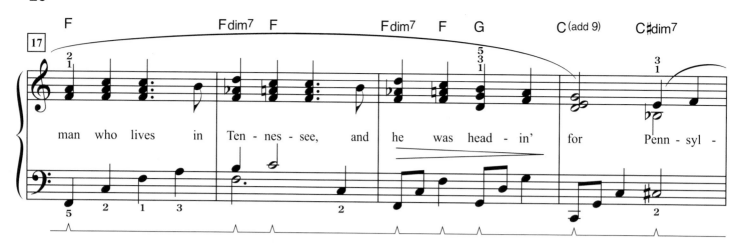

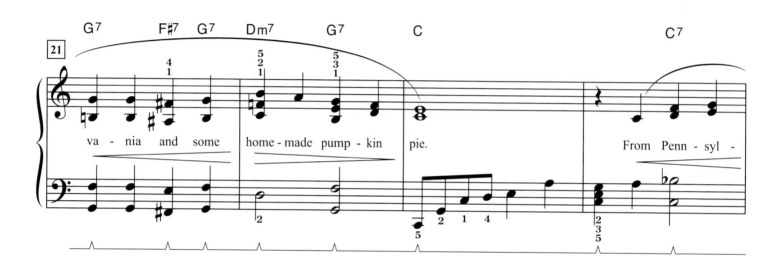

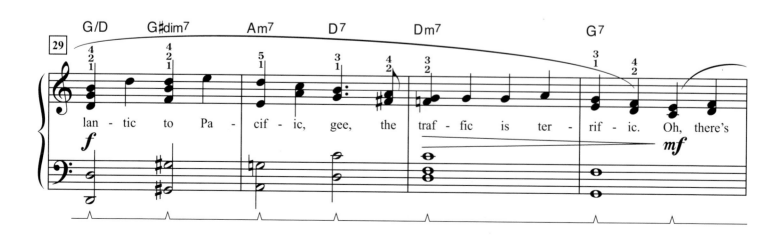

# I'll Be Home for Christmas

Words by Kim Gannon
Music by Walter Kent
Arr. Mike Springer

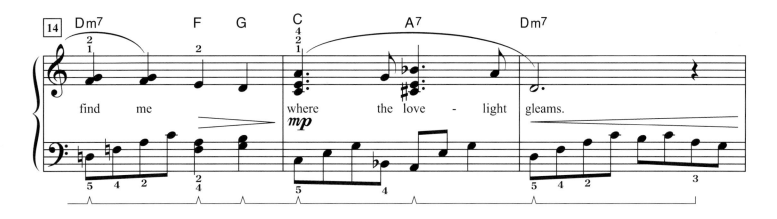

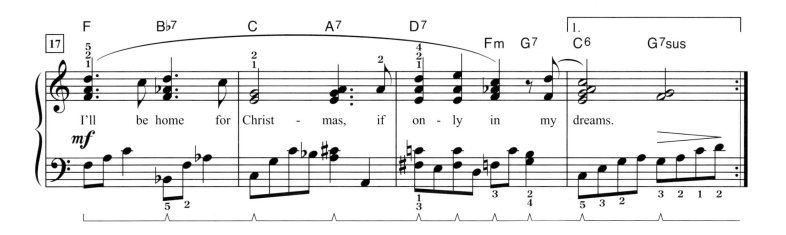

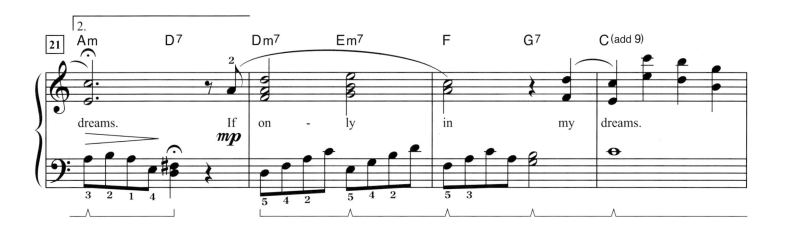

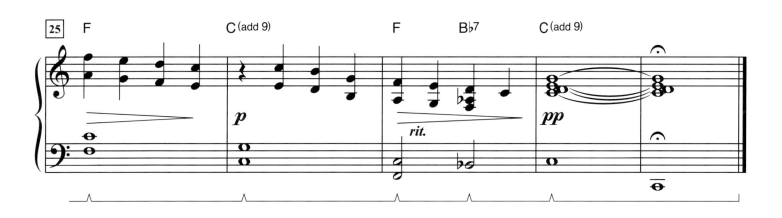

# It's the Most Wonderful Time of the Year

Words and Music by
Eddie Pola and George Wyle
Arr. Mike Springer

# Jingle Bell Rock

Words and Music by
Joe Beal and Jim Boothe
Arr. Mike Springer

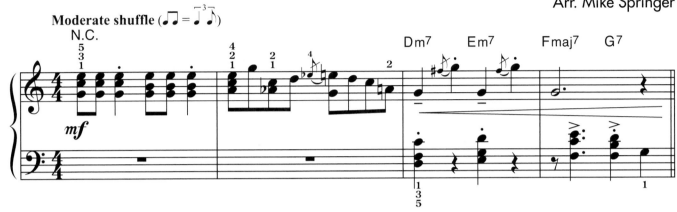

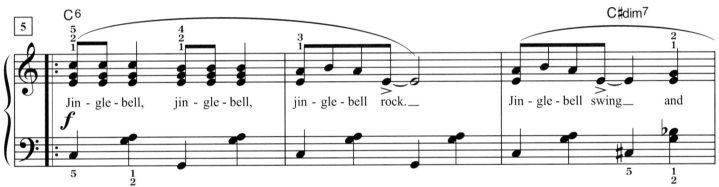

LH quarters detached throughout

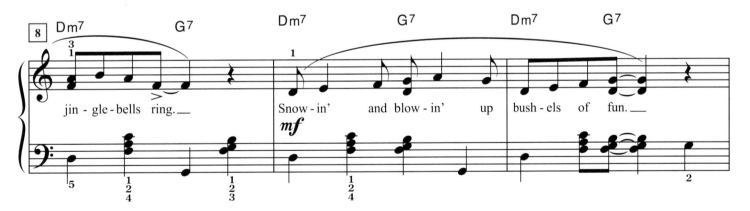

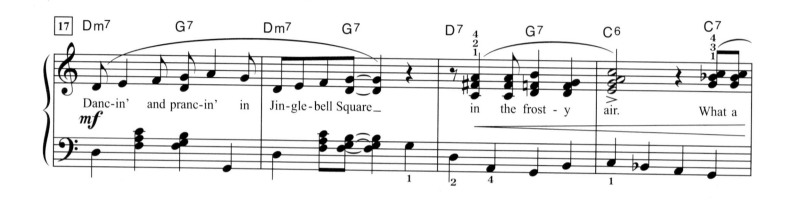

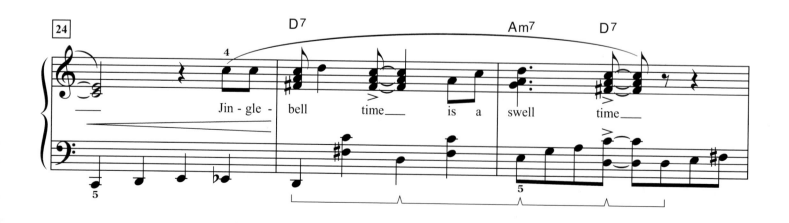

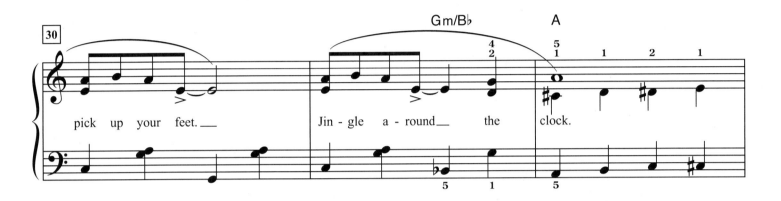

# Let It Snow! Let It Snow! Let It Snow!

Words by Sammy Cahn
Music by Jule Styne
Arr. Mike Springer

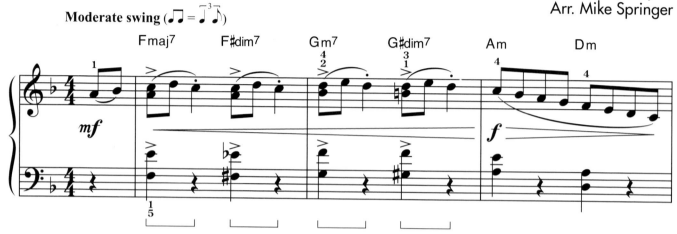

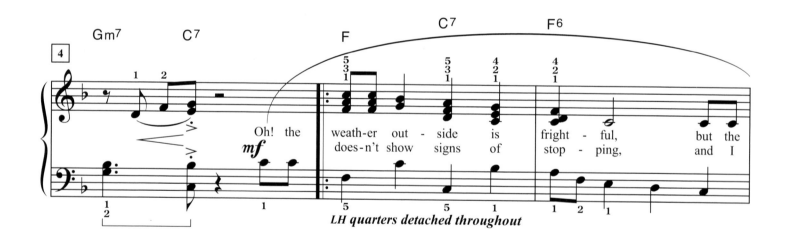

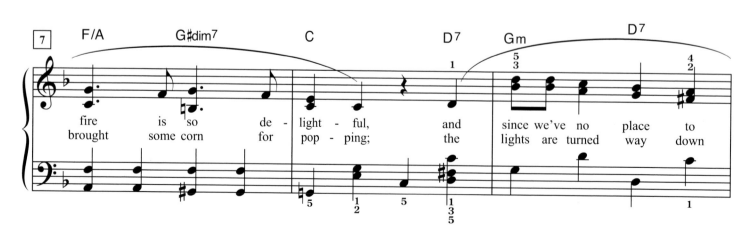

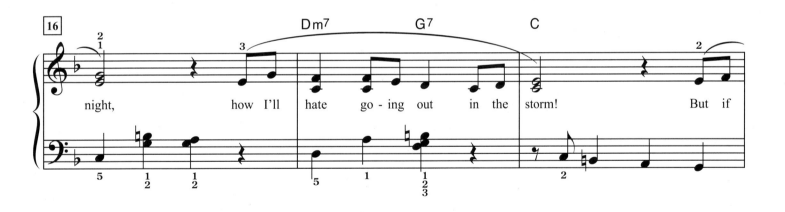

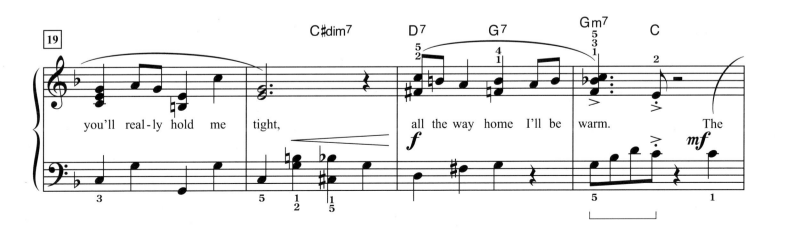

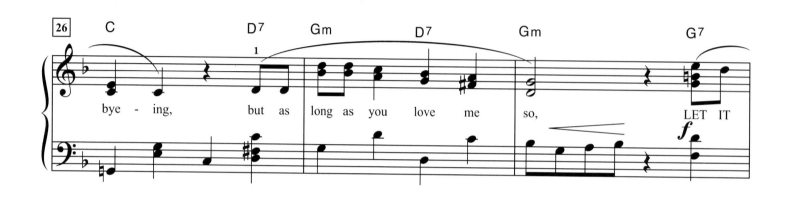

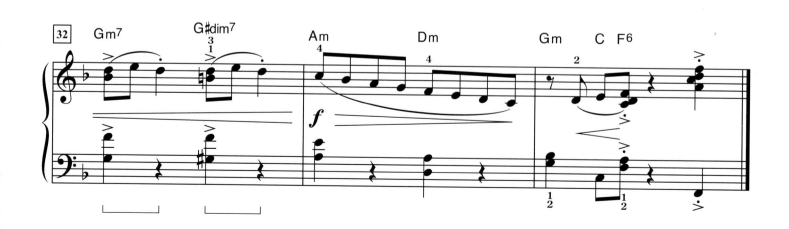

# Rockin' Around the Christmas Tree

Words and Music by Johnny Marks
Arr. Mike Springer

# Rudolph, the Red-Nosed Reindeer

Words and Music by Johnny Marks
Arr. Mike Springer

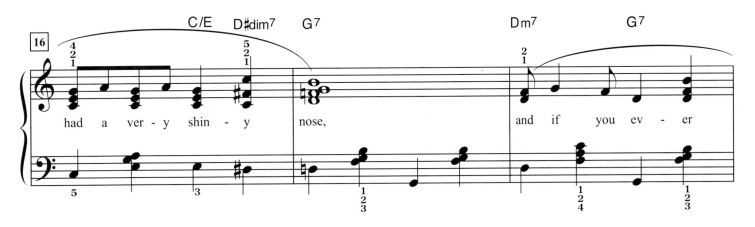

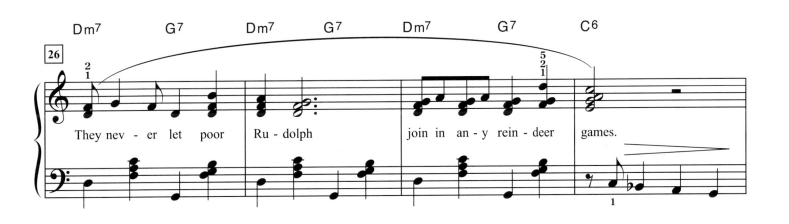

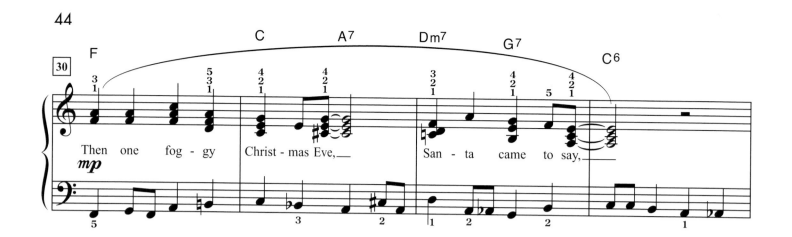

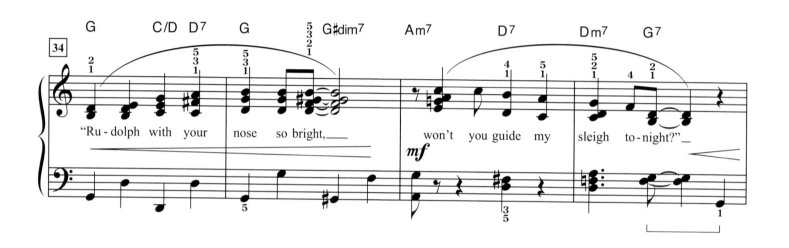

# Santa Baby

Words and Music by Joan Javits,
Philip Springer and Tony Springer
Arr. Mike Springer

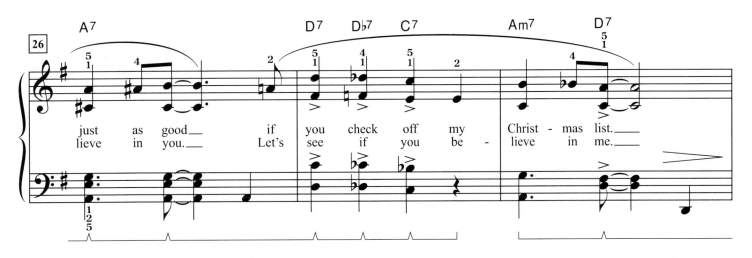

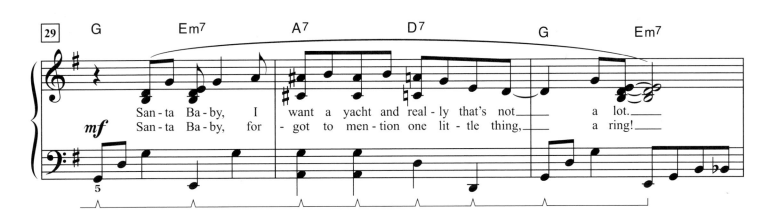

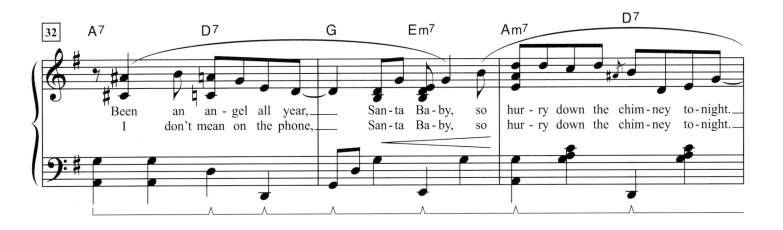

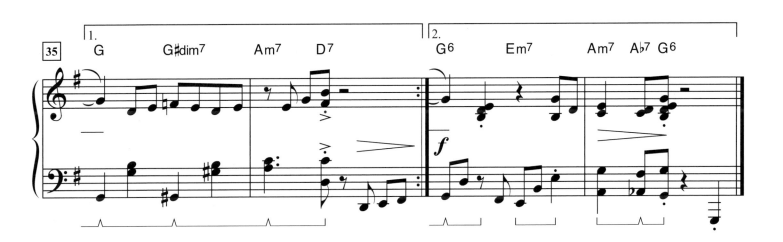

# Santa Claus Is Comin' to Town

Words by Haven Gillespie
Music by J. Fred Coots
Arr. Mike Springer

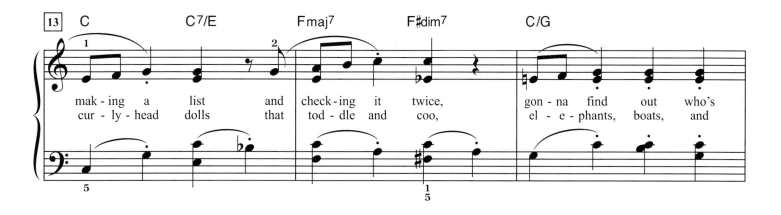

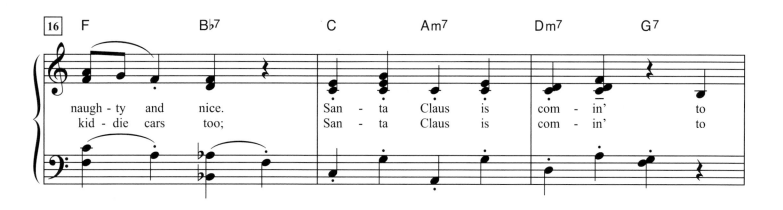

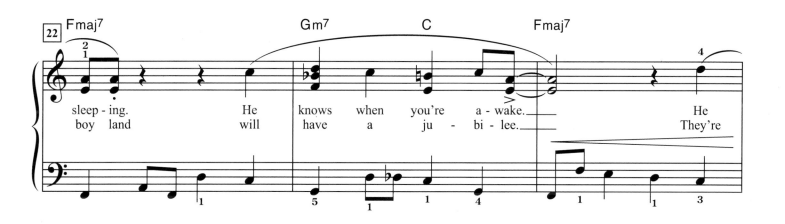

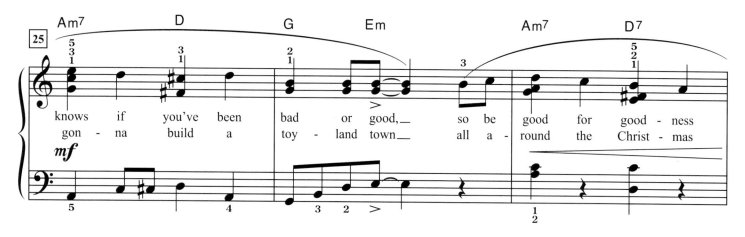

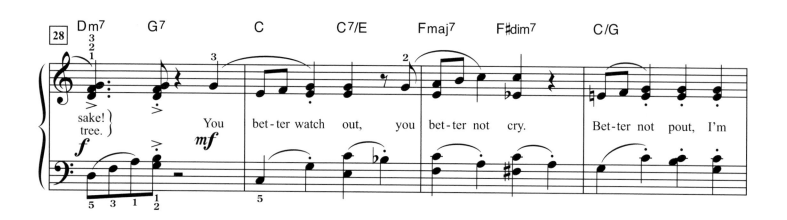

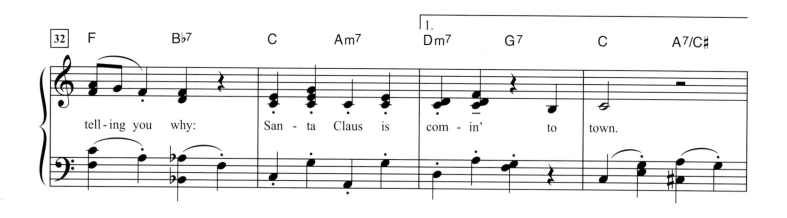

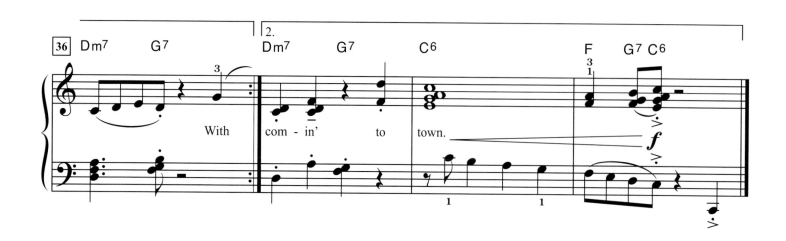

# Sleigh Ride

Music by Leroy Anderson
Words by Mitchell Parish
Arr. Mike Springer

52

# Silver and Gold

Words and Music by Johnny Marks
Arr. Mike Springer

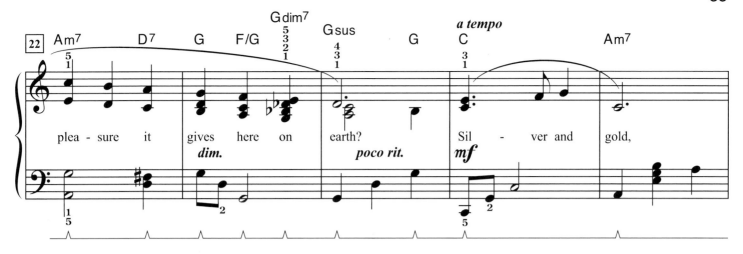

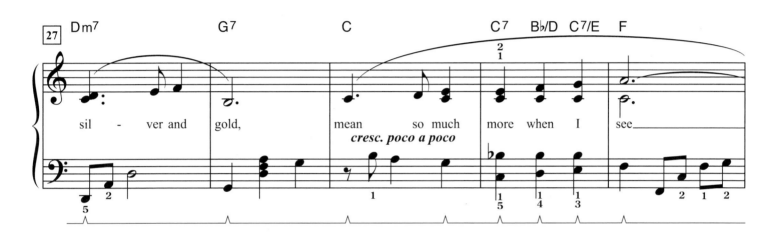

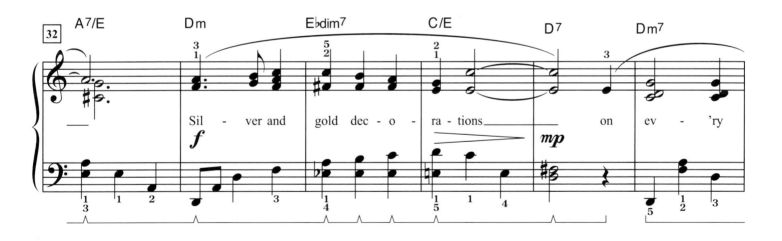

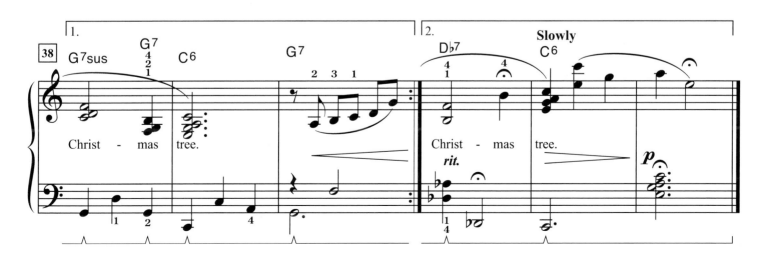

# Toyland

Music by Victor Herbert
Lyrics by Glen MacDonough
Arr. Mike Springer

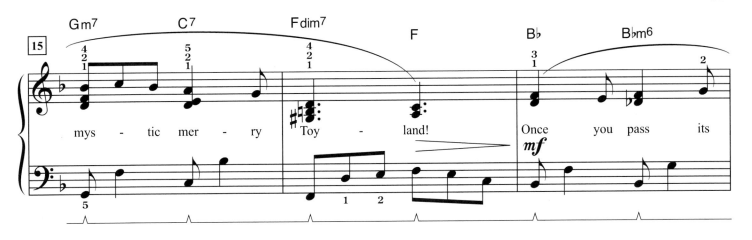

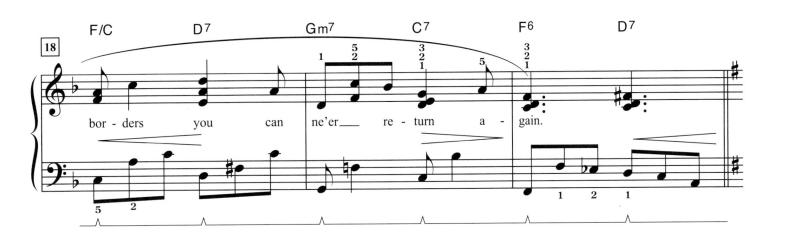

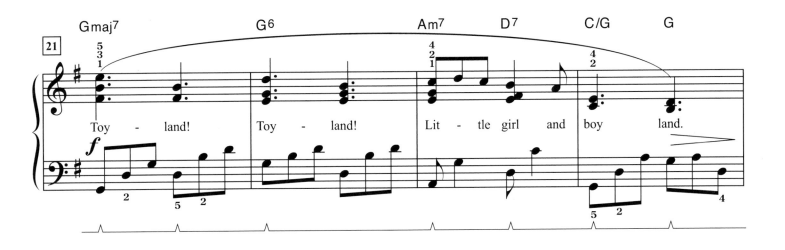

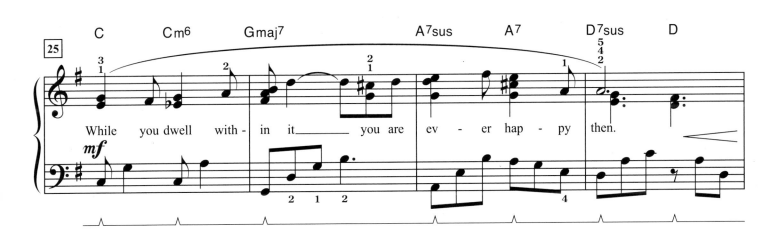

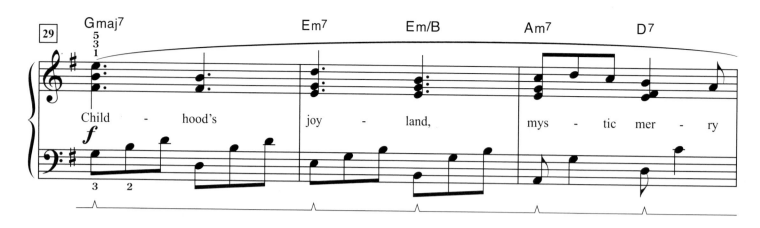

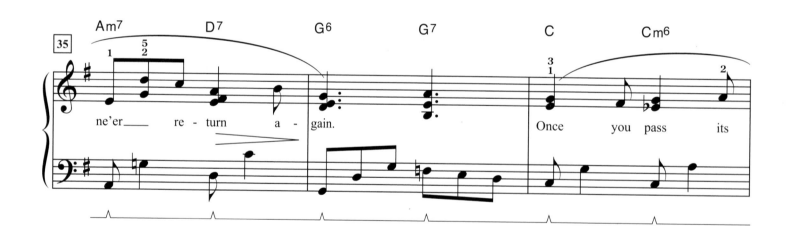

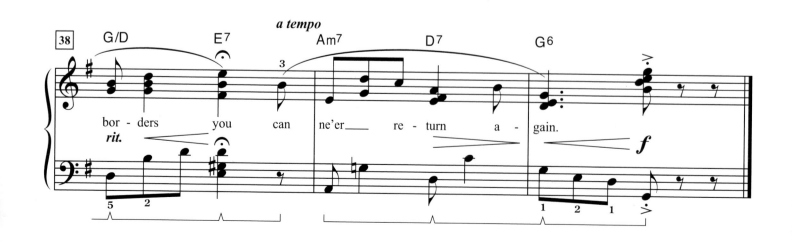

# Winter Wonderland

Words by Dick Smith
Music by Felix Bernard
Arr. Mike Springer

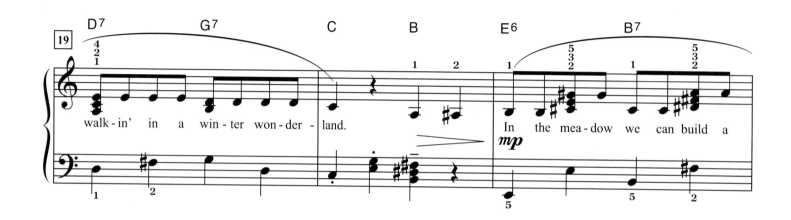

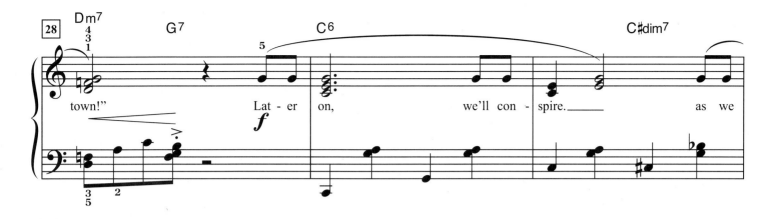

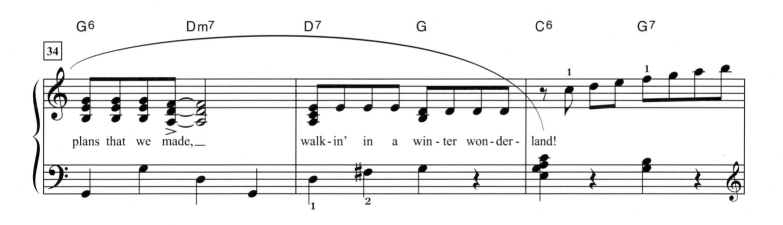

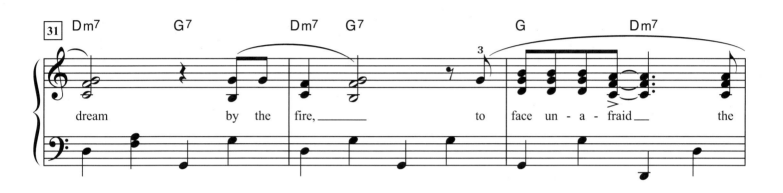

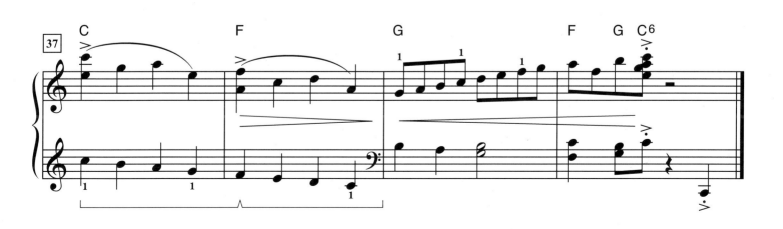

# You're a Mean One, Mr. Grinch

Music by Albert Hague
Lyrics by Dr. Seuss
Arr. Mike Springer